Lost Houses of the West Riding

EDWARD WATERSON & PETER MEADOWS

Foreword by John Harris

HEATH OLD HALL · 24935 JY

Heath Old Hall

JILL RAINES
1998

GH00496885

FOREWORD
by
John Harris Curator Emeritus of the R.I.B.A. Drawings Collection

When Marcus Binney and I were preparing the ground for the *Destruction of the Country House* exhibition held at the Victoria and Albert Museum under Roy Strong's encouraging directorship from 1974, we were at a loss for statistics on demolitions. This information had never been systematically collected on a county basis. We were obliged to use the red box library of the National Monuments Record in liaison with Peter Reid and Derek Sherborn, the only lost house experts who had actually attempted to tabulate losses in any detailed way. We therefore resorted to local authorities whose response was varied. Some had half a dozen so-called "lost houses" within their boundaries, but knew not if they were there! In the short preparation time granted us we could only make limited excursions of discovery. We also communicated with local newspapers, librarians and historians. This led to very interesting results, not least that newspapers were thirsty for information. They queried our interest and demanded to know the importance of the house. This exchange was one of the incentives for Marcus to found SAVE Britain's Heritage and its weapon of the press notice.

We did our best but it was not enough. We needed local enthusiasts to establish what survived on the site after demolition - and so much did. Pevsner in all his counties was neglectful of this, assuming quite wrongly that if the house had gone, not much remained. Precious time was of the essence for him too. We needed site descriptions of the sort that SAVE was able to acquire for its *Lost Houses of Scotland,* July 1980, or Tom Lloyd for SAVE's *The Lost Houses of Wales*, September 1986. These reflected a curiosity in the building history of the whole estate.

Marcus and I believe our exhibition to have been a catalyst for a younger generation of regional historians to attend to what we left out. Suddenly the counties are being investigated. The north of England has particularly benefitted from enthusiasts. I refer to *Lost Houses of East Yorkshire* by David Neave and Edward Waterson, 1988; to Waterson and Peter Meadows's *Lost Houses of York and the North Riding,* 1990, and their *Lost Houses of County Durham,* 1993; Thomas Faulkner and Phoebe Lowery's *Lost Houses of Newcastle and Northumberland,* 1996; and Terence Leach and Robert Pacey's two volumes of *Lost Houses of Lincolnshire,* 1990 and 1993, with their extensive family histories.

Now we have Waterson and Meadows's *Lost Houses of the West Riding,* and what excitement this causes me! I will be fascinated to read their lists of losses. How tragically these lists have lengthened since 1974. Then we listed 19 losses for Derbyshire. Recently that number has been increased by 26. In 1974 the total loss for the British Isles was about 750. Today statistics demonstrate that this awful tally must be at least doubled, to somewhere near 2000.

During my adolescence I was peripatetic, as related in *No Voice From The Hall: Early Memories of a Country House Snooper,* 1998. I bitterly regret that my youth hostelling forays rarely took me as far as Yorkshire. I did see Halnaby Hall, the amazing Kippax Park, Scriven Hall before the fire, and Whitley Beaumont from a distance. I wish I had been more curious to infiltrate myself into Whitley, a noble baroque house with James Paine decorations. I hope this new book with encourage historians in other counties to do likewise.

INTRODUCTION

"There are few parts of England, of the same extent, that contain a greater number of noblemen and gentlemen's seats, than the West Riding of Yorkshire"
John Bigland (1819).

It is the date of Bigland's pronouncement that is significant. When we set out to compile this volume, we expected the typical West Riding lost house to be a product of the late nineteenth century and probably of dubious architectural merit. But as Bigland points out, the West Riding was well provided with country houses in 1800, and the majority of important lost houses dated from the eighteenth and early nineteenth centuries. The typical Victorian industrialist built a sizeable villa close to the source of his wealth, but his successors aspired to something grander and acquired an estate in the still rural heartlands of the West Riding.

The West Riding was far more than today's West Yorkshire, centring on Bradford, Dewsbury, Leeds, Halifax, Huddersfield and Wakefield. It was one of the three historic divisions of Yorkshire, and by far the largest (it was larger than any other English county). It included today's South Yorkshire, Barnsley, Doncaster, Rotherham and Sheffield, it took in large areas of Wharfedale and Nidderdale now in the rural county of North Yorkshire, and it spilled over the Pennines to cover the forest of Bowland, now in Lancashire, and Sedbergh and district, now part of Cumbria.

Industrialisation was superimposed on an earlier society which had already built its country houses. For a while these eighteenth century houses thrived on this new nineteenth century wealth, although

Kiveton Hall was demolished as early as 1800. In time, however, and especially in the south-east of the West Riding, mining and industry so ruined the environment that owners like the Earls of Mexborough at Methley Hall were only too glad to sell up and move out. In some cases the mining beneath the houses literally precipitated their downfall. The central section of Byram Hall, including Robert Adam's library, collapsed after being undermined, leaving just the two wings standing. Fire, indiscriminate in its victims, gutted several houses including Studley Royal in 1946 and Scriven Hall in 1952. Creeping urbanisation in the heavily populated central and southern parts of the West Riding led to the demolition of halls and villas as early as 1900. A modest country house like Potternewton Hall was too near Leeds to avoid becoming Riviera Gardens in the 1930's.

Further out, houses already unmanageable in the years of recession in the 1920's and 1930's were so thoroughly abused during wartime requisitioning that they could not be reoccupied afterwards. In the dark years of the 1950's the West Riding was no exception to John Harris's observation that a major country house was being demolished every two and a half days. In some areas, notably Huddersfield and Sheffield, new uses were found for most of these old warhorses. More recently the method pioneered by Kit Martin has been followed in Yorkshire, and even the most unwieldy houses, such as Kirklees Hall, have had their future assured by being split vertically into private houses.

Our greatest problem, in so large and heavily populated an area as the West Riding, was which demolished houses should be omitted. We have therefore

concentrated on the larger lost houses, and tried to include something from every part of the West Riding. Surprisingly, perhaps, the largest and grandest houses have often been the least well recorded. The names of famous architects, Burlington, Paine, Carr and others, occur occasionally in our pages, but all too often the names of the architects and craftsmen who built the West Riding's great houses are not recorded. Louis Ambler's admirable *The Old Halls and Manor Houses of Yorkshire,* published as long ago as 1913, remains the standard work on the subject, and he managed to record many of these older and more modest houses before they went. In a sense, he did the job for us nearly a century ago and our task has been to record the eighteenth and nineteenth century losses.

The principles of inclusion are as in previous volumes in this series. Mediaeval castles have been excluded, as have most houses ruined for centuries. Houses demolished before 1900 and not rebuilt on the same site are described, as are houses lost since 1900, even where a new house was built on the site. A few houses of exceptional interest, which have been substantially reduced, such as Ingmire Hall, have also been included.

The houses have been arranged geographically, starting at the north-west corner, working east, then through the central conurbation down to what is now South Yorkshire.

It is inevitable that many houses will have been omitted, either because we did not know about them or because we had not space to include them. We would be most grateful to receive information about them, and we would appreciate the loan (for copying) of additional or better photographs of any of the houses which we have featured.

3

INGMIRE HALL,
near Sedburgh

Situated close to Sedburgh, in a part of the West Riding across the Pennines since 1974 part of Cumbria, Ingmire Hall was a rambling Tudor-style house, part ancient, part enlarged in 1838, probably by George Webster of Kendal. It was the seat of Sir John Otway, who played an important role in English history in the 17th century during the Commonwealth. Later it was the residence of the Upton family. John Upton (1800-43) was the rebuilder. *The Westmorland Gazette* reported on 2nd January 1844 that "The house has recently undergone a state of complete repair, is newly furnished... The stables, coach house and offices are quite new." The most extraordinary feature was the turreted and castellated curtain wall at the rear, giving the impression of fortifications. In 1897 Mrs. Upton-Cottrell-Dormer was the owner, in 1922 Major John H. Upton. In that year he decided to sell up. The contents, including a fine collection of old china, were sold between 27th June and 1st July 1922, and the Hall was sold by auction on 4th August. A few years later, in 1928, it was burnt. Ingmire was partially reconstructed by Sir T. Strickland.

(1) Ingmire Hall (Angus Taylor)

(2) Ingmire Hall, side view (Angus Taylor)

Ingmire Hall, aerial view (R. Hayhurst)

HELLIFIELD PEEL,
Long Preston

Hellifield Peel was the seat of the Hamertons for over 400 years.

Lawrence Hamerton received royal licence to embattle Hellifield in 1440. It was a sturdy fortified retreat with walls of great thickness. The windows were Georgianised in the 18th century, when it is probable that the lower wing was added. In 1900 it was the property of Chisnall Hamerton of Sunderland, and the seat of Frank B. Wright.

Later it was the home of Sir William Nicholson, builder; but now it is partially demolished.

Hellifield Peel (R. Hayhurst)

GLEDSTONE HALL,
Marton-in-Craven

Gledstone, in upper Airedale north-west of Skipton, was a house of c.1770 designed (most probably) by John Carr of York for Richard Roundell (1740-72) and finished for William Roundell (1742-1821), his brother and heir. It stood on an elevated site and commanded fine views of Craven. The main house was a square block with a central canted bay, and curved flights of steps rose to the entrance in this bay. The main rooms were on the first floor. The house was flanked by smaller, two-bay pavilions, and to one side was the large stable block (which survives), with a domed lantern tower over the entrance, and inside a circular court surrounded by an arcaded ambulatory. Richard Roundell was the owner in 1897. About 1922 Sir Amos Nelson acquired Gledstone, and at first intended to extend the Hall, which had cramped and inconvenient accommodation. Later he decided to build a new house on higher ground, and in 1925-27 Gledstone was demolished and replaced with a distinguished house by Sir Edwin Lutyens. Some of the doors and fine fireplaces from old Gledstone were re-used in Lutyens' house.

(1) Gledstone Hall (plate from Whitaker's Craven, 3rd ed. 1878)

(2) Gledstone Hall (R. Hayhurst)

CONISTON HALL,
Coniston Cold

Coniston Hall in upper Airedale was prettily situated beside a 25-acre lake. Various families held the estate: the Malhams until 1665, the Coulthursts of Gargrave, and the Laycocks of Lotherdale from c.1720. Coniston was bought by J.B. Garforth in 1812, and in 1841 he commissioned George Webster of Kendal to design a new house. It was a handsome classical building with a three-bay pediment on the garden or lake side, and a six-column Greek Doric portico on the entrance side. The house passed to the Tottie family. James Braithwaite Garforth Tottie was the owner in 1897 and as long as 1922. After the death of Richard Tottie, Coniston Hall was offered for sale in 1969 and demolished in 1972, except for the portico, which was incorporated into a new house built on the site.

(1) Coniston Hall, entrance front (RCHME)

(2) Coniston Hall, garden front (R. Hayhurst)

(3) Coniston Hall (Whitaker's Craven)

BOLTON HALL,
Bolton-by-Bowland

Bolton Hall stood above the River Ribble in what is now Lancashire but until 1974 was part of the West Riding. It was an ancient hall extensively remodelled for John Bolton c.1808, with large additions later in the 19th century. Henry VI sheltered at Bolton after the Battle of Hexham in 1464. A room was shown which was said to have been his, and in the grounds was 'King Henry's Well', supposedly discovered by Henry during his stay, and over which a well-head was erected. Samuel Buck's drawing of Bolton, c.1720, shows a plain, H-shaped building with mostly 17th century square-headed windows, with a few Gothic windows remaining from the medieval house. Bishop Pococke, in his journey through England in 1751, visited Bolton and was shown a pair of boots said to have been King Henry's, "of yellow tanned leather, lined with fur and buttoned up the sides." Other 18th century commentators observed that the high table in the great hall still had a canopy of state over it. John Bolton of Liverpool bought the estate in 1808 for £42,000 and commissioned J.M. Gandy to repair and rebuild the house. Most of the external detail, the Gothic-style windows, the round turrets and the castellations, were Gandy's. A little later, in 1808-11, he remodelled Storrs Hall in Westmorland

(1) Bolton Hall (J. Davidson)

(2) Bolton Hall, dining room (R. Hayhurst)

8

(3) Above: Bolton Hall, dining room wing (R. Hayhurst)
(4) Bolton Hall, interior (R. Hayhurst)

also for John Bolton, where his executant architect was George Webster of Kendal. Bolton sold Bolton Hall c.1830. By 1897 Charles Booth Elmsall Wright owned the estate, and large Victorian Gothic additions, primarily a new dining room, were made. In 1922 he was still the owner, but the Hall was unoccupied. Bolton Hall, after falling into disrepair, was demolished c.1959.

FLASBY HALL,
near Skipton

Flasby was an Italianate mansion of 1843-44 by George Webster of Kendal for Cooper Preston (1786-1860). It was a square classical block with hipped roof and pediments, only slightly Victorian in its detailing, but with an Italianate tower, with an open, arched belvedere. In 1922 it was the seat of John Henry Preston, and the residence of Thomas Howarth. By 1988 it was mostly in ruins, having been vandalised and burnt, and the tower was gone. It has been rebuilt as a smaller house.

Flasby Hall (Angus Taylor)

BEWERLEY HALL,
Pateley Bridge

Mary, Lady Yorke, widow of Sir John Yorke (1633-63), bought the manor of Bewerley in 1674 for her son Thomas Yorke (1658-1716). His grandson John Yorke (1733-1813) spent much time at Bewerley after succeeding his father in 1768. He began the transformation of the house from its old, plain form. On the east side he built two of the round corner towers, and added a morning room and a room above it. He laid out the park with walks, and on top of the hill near Guisecliffe built an arched ruin called The Folly. John Yorke left most of his property away from his nephew and heir John Yorke (1776-1851), who was forced to sell his property in Richmond, including his town house, The Green (see *Lost Houses of York and the North Riding*). He made Bewerley his main residence. The dilapidated hall was repaired and enlarged between 1815 and 1821. Another round tower was added, and all the towers received conical turrets. Further alterations were made in 1832 by Anthony Salvin, some inspired by suggestions from Lord Ribblesdale of Gisburn Park. The rooms included a study, drawing room, dining room, ballroom, morning room, library and eighteen bedrooms. John Yorke's two

(1) Bewerley Hall (D. Yorke)

(2) Bewerley Hall, entrance front (D. Yorke)

sons had the estate next: John Yorke (1827-83) and Thomas Yorke (1832-1923). The latter made changes about 1904: a ballroom and smoking room were created in the old laundry, and an elaborately carved Jacobean oak overmantel was bought from Hunwick Hall and installed there. Thomas Yorke was succeeded by his grandson John Yorke (1904-96), whose mother, alarmed about finance in the slump after the First World War, ordered Bewerley to be sold. The estate was split up, and the hall was sold for its materials and demolished in 1923.

The sale raised £150,000 and speculators resold the site of the hall for a huge profit.

(3) Bewerley Hall, aerial view (D. Yorke)

GOUTHWAITE HALL

The site of Gouthwaite Hall, a seat of the Yorkes of Bewerley from the 16th century, lies beneath Gouthwaite Reservoir in upper Nidderdale. It was submerged c.1900. It was a Tudor style building with many mullioned and transomed windows. In the late 19th century it was divided into three houses for tenants. Some of the stone, an old chimneypiece and Jacobean oak panelling, were re-used in a new hunting lodge for the Yorkes built on higher ground in 1901.

Gouthwaite Hall (Anne Ashley-Cooper, Yorke Country)

STUDLEY ROYAL,
near Ripon

Studley Royal is one of the finest landscape estates in England, including in its bounds the stupendous Gothic eye-catcher of Fountains Abbey; but the great house of the Aislabies and the Vyners was demolished following a devastating fire on 13th April 1946. The two estates were united in the late 18th century, when William Aislabie bought the adjoining Fountains Hall and ruins. Studley Royal was held directly from the Crown, and passed in descent from Henry II's reign, often through the female line. George Aislabie, a South Yorkshire lawyer, married the heiress of the Mallory family, owners since 1444, in the mid-17th century. His second son John Aislabie succeeded his brother in 1699. He held a string of lucrative government appointments and was Chancellor of the Exchequer 1718-20. A strong supporter of the South Sea Company project, when the 'Bubble' burst in 1720 he was made a scapegoat, was tried, deprived of his offices and imprisoned in the Tower; but he kept his possessions and money, and retired to his estate of Studley Royal. In 1716 the Tudor house, shown in a drawing as a traditional gabled house with a deeply recessed centre and projecting wings, was severely damaged by fire. Aislabie

(1) Studley Royal (Country Life)

(2) Studley Royal (Walter Scott (Bradford) Ltd)

filled the centre with a two-storeyed entrance hall, to which his son added a portico and other Gothick embellishments in 1762. Aislabie knew Vanbrugh, working at Castle Howard, but there is no suggestion that Vanbrugh had a hand in the design of Studley Royal; indeed, slight indications suggest that Aislabie might have been his own architect. There are references to Doe, Aislabie's mason, being called to Castle Howard in 1734. The hall, originally two-storeyed, was altered about 1910, when a ceiling was put in, panelling added, and bedrooms made above. Behind the hall, the staircase hall had fine plasterwork on its walls, possibly by Nadaud and Cortese, for there was identical plasterwork at Gilling Castle, Yorkshire, where they were known to have worked. The dining room ceiling also closely resembled work at Gilling. William Aislabie died in 1781 and Studley Royal descended through the female line until 1845, when it was inherited by the 2nd Earl de Grey (d.1859), and from him by his brother, the 1st Earl of Ripon. His son (d.1907) was Viceroy of India 1880-84 and was created 1st Marquess of Ripon. He added a Gothic chapel to the west of the house. His son, the 2nd Marquess, died in 1923 and was succeeded by Clare Vyner, grandson of a daughter of the 1st Earl de Grey. He was the owner when the house burnt down in 1946, and later converted the stable block into a new house.

(3) Studley Royal, dining room, formerly the library (Country Life)

(4) Studley Royal, staircase (Country Life)
(5) Studley Royal, chimneypiece of the East room (Country Life)

SCRIVEN HALL,
Knaresborough

Scriven, an early 18th century house of considerable architectural importance, was destroyed by fire in 1952. The Slingsby family were the owners from the mid-14th century. The old house was described by the diarist Henry Slingsby as "that rotten house at Scriving" and Warburton commented on its ancient character c.1718. All was changed by Sir Henry Slingsby, when the main front was remodelled and a new facade built, to designs of William Wakefield, Yorkshire gentleman architect. Slingsby's sister married Thomas Duncombe of Duncombe Park, Helmsley, and Wakefield was the architect there. The carpenter was William Etty, York carpenter and architect. The heavy Ionic portico was enclosed and formed part of the entrance hall, with windows with heavy Gibbs surrounds. The last male, Sir Charles Slingsby (1824-69) was drowned when a ferry capsized in the Ure. He had been hunting with the York and Ainsty. Scriven passed to his sister, and after her death in 1899 to the Revd. Charles Slingsby Atkinson, who assumed the Slingsby name and arms. In December 1952 it was being cleaned after several years disuse following army occupation in the 1939-45 War, when fire broke out. The Fire Protection Association recorded some of the ruined rooms, but its photographs are lost.

(1) Scriven Hall (Walter Scott (Bradford) Ltd)
(2) Scriven Hall, (W.H. Scott, The West Riding... at the opening of the 20th century, 1902)

KIRBY HALL,
Little Ouseburn

When Kirby Hall was demolished in the early 1920's, the West Riding lost one of its most important houses which was, at least in part, designed by the Earl of Burlington.

Stephen Thompson first approached Col. James Moyser, a gifted amateur architect, in1746. Moyser in turn suggested he consult the London architect Roger Morris, who drew up plans, assisted by Lord Burlington.

Work commenced, with Thompson very much in charge but as early as 1748 he wrote "I have got a clever young fellow of a mason at the head of my works". That clever young fellow was John Carr. By the time the house had been finished in 1756 Carr had designed many of the finishing touches to the interior. Rich plasterwork in the gallery was by Thomas Perritt of York and in the dining room by Guiseppe Cortese, both of whom were to be closely associated with Carr in future years. Carving by Grinling Gibbons and paintings by Thornhill were said to have come from Canons.

The end result was illustrated in *Vitruvius Britannicus* with a note that "the plan is distinguished as well for its elegance as for its utility". That was perhaps just as well, considering the cost amounted to £13,500. Tradition relates that in view of the expense, Thompson refused to finish the gallery, although he could still find £1,500 to spend on furnishings.

Outside, J.B. Papworth landscaped the park and added a conservatory in 1833. In 1857 the eight-roomed wing built in 1800 was pulled down and replaced with a 24-roomed version, completed in 1860. Paxton built hothouses in 1863; a very pretty lodge, now derelict, was probably to the designs of Robert Lugar.

Kirby Hall (RCHME)

Kirby Hall, drawing room (RCHME)

15

GREEN HAMMERTON HALL

An early twentieth century map shows Green Hammerton Hall as having built on the site of an old manor house and it must certainly have started its life as something rather more simple than the jumbled piece of architecture that eventually emerged.

Although its early history is unclear, the Dowager Lady Clifford carried out enlargements after her purchase of the estate in 1809. In 1853 the Reverend Richard Ridley left the house to his nephew Henry Richard Farrer and it was Farrer who carried out extensive works between 1867 and 1878. These included a new mansard roof to the main block and a chateauesque tower.

It was demolished in 1952.

Green Hammerton Hall (N. Hetherton)

WETHERBY GRANGE

Bielby Thompson obtained plans from "the Great Mr. Wyatt" and had them amended by John Carr. This most distinctive house had a large three-storey circular tower to the main elevation. The estate devolved by marriage to the Thompsons of Escrick then by sale, in 1856, to the trustees of Robert Gunter as a surprise present for his son on his return from the Crimean War.

A sale catalogue of 1941 offered the house as Lot 61, "temporarily occupied by H. M. Government". It stipulated that if the house were bought for demolition the site had to be cleared within six months.

In fact it survived until 1964.

The Grange (J. Davidson)

WIGHILL PARK

When the Stapletons bought the estate in 1376 they replaced the pele tower of the Haget and Turet families with a wood and stone manor house. In 1580, Sir Robert Stapleton built an Elizabethan house, which included an elaborately carved doorway, now incorporated in the farmhouse which stands at the entrance to the park.

Henry Stapleton died in 1779 but his daughter Martha married Captain Granville Chetwynd, who assumed the name Chetwynd-Stapleton and was responsible for the building of an ashlar-fronted house on a rise in the park. The old house was demolished.

In 1811 the new house was sold to Fountayne Wilson MP.

During the tenancy of the Lords Hawke, Wighill Park reached its zenith and in 1886 they improved and enlarged it. The seventh Lord Hawke, captain of Yorkshire from 1883 to 1910, left in 1924.

In the 1950's the estate was split and sold. The house and grounds were stripped of the standing timber and most of the building materials. The shell was bought by an architect, who formed a new bungalow from the remains. The stables, with an attractive cupola, still stand.

(1) Elizabethan house,1779 (H Speight. Lower Wharfedale)

(2) South Front (A Wright)

HEALAUGH MANOR, Tadcaster

Benjamin Brooksbank built Healaugh Manor for his wife, who complained their old house was dirty and damp. Family tradition links John Carr with the design.

In a commanding position overlooking the River Wharfe, it had the unusual distinction of having a deer park over the river, which necessitated the building of a wooden bridge with stone parapets to link house and park.

It was restored by Edward Brooksbank following a fire in 1901 but was said to be in a poor state of repair when it failed to reach its reserve at auction on 15th August 1944. It was demolished soon afterwards.

Healaugh Manor (Tadcaster Historical Society)

POPPLETON HALL, Nether Poppleton

A pleasant Georgian house that began life as The Villa. John Fothergill offered it for sale in 1797, when it was described as "modern", so he may well have been the builder.

The three-acre grounds ran down to the Ouse and were laid out as pleasure gardens, with a spring that doubled up as a cold bath and ornament.

Later inhabitants included Isaac Spencer, twice Lord Mayor of York, and Sir Newbald Kaye, who played host to Lloyd George.

It became a convalescent home after the war and was demolished in the 1960's, to make way for Poppleton Hall Gardens.

Poppleton Hall (A. Williams)

18

APPLETON HOUSE,
Nun Appleton

Forming part of the Nun Appleton estate but not to be confused with Nun Appleton Hall, which still stands, this house probably dated from the time of Lord Holden's purchase of the estate from the Milner family in 1894.

Very red brick but with lashings of oak, it was still in its youth when it appeared as Lot 27 in the sale catalogue of 1913.

Thought to have been a school between the wars, it was back in the saleroom in 1936, this time on behalf of Mr Douglas Banks.

It was demolished shortly after the Second World War.

Appleton House (1913 Sale Catalogue)

SCARTHINGWELL HALL,
near Tadcaster

The seventeenth century house of the Hamonds was incorporated into the later houses built by their successors and survived as servants quarters (minus its gables) right up to the demolition of the house in about 1960.

In the meantime the estate had passed by marriage to Lord Hawke who, in 1848, sold it to the Maxwell family. They added a new south wing and a huge Catholic church, modelled on the Chapel Royal at Munich. The architects were J. B. and W. Atkinson.

The Maxwells sold up in 1948 and the house was in a ruinous state for years. The church survives.

Scarthingwell Hall

PARLINGTON HALL,
Aberford

The Gascoignes had owned Parlington from 1546 and Sir Thomas's classical house probably incorporated the earlier house illustrated in Buck's sketchbook. Various plans to replace it with something grander came to nought but a triumphal arch celebrating "Liberty in North America Triumphant" was built from stone intended for the new house. This arch caused the non-visit of the Prince Regent who, on hearing of the inscription, refused to join the Gascoignes for lunch. It was abandoned in the early years of the century, ruinous by 1952 and finally went some years later. The park, including the arch, remains largely intact.

Parlington House (J. Davidson)

SWILLINGTON HOUSE

The Lowthers bought the Swillington estate in 1663 and built a new house in the 1690's. In about 1738 Sir William Lowther employed Henry Flitcroft to rebuild the principal rooms and staircase. The house itself was rebuilt (or perhaps more accurately extended) in 1803/4 with a large stable block and a walled garden that was reputed to have used a million bricks. The park was stocked with rare trees that the family had brought from all corners of the world.

Sir Charles Lowther sold the house to a colliery company who undermined it, leading to its demolition in 1950.

Swillington House (J. Davidson)

20

KIPPAX PARK,
Castleford

Kippax Park was bought by Thomas Bland of Castleford in 1595. His Elizabethan house of nine bays on three floors seems to have had a quiet life for the next 150 years, despite the burgeoning wealth of the Blands.

The excitement really started when John Bland, the sixth baronet and a notorious gambler, inherited the estate in 1743.

Around 1750 over £8000 was spent on extending the house to designs now attributed to Daniel Garrett. The main house was embellished with two large canted bays with ogee roofs and window heads but the most striking thing about the enlarged Kippax was the sheer length of it. Weighing in at 37 bays and around 600 feet in length, it ranked among the longest of English country houses, which encouraged Sir John to wager a bet with the Wentworths of Wentworth Woodhouse that his was the longer of the two houses. He lost by a short head.

In 1755 he lost £32,000 in one night's gambling and fled to France, subsequently committing suicide.

John Davison Bland was the last member of the family to live at the house and died without an heir in 1928. There was a six day sale of the contents in 1929, following which it was abandoned. Already derelict by 1953, it was removed over a period of years as open cast coal mining crept across the park.

Kippax Park (RCHME)

Kippax Park (RCHME)

BYRAM PARK,
Ferrybridge

The Ramsdens were a Huddersfield dynasty who bought the Byram estate in 1612. Buck (1720) shows a sixteenth century house with what appear to have been Ramsden embellishments.

In the late seventeenth century Huddersfield prospered on the back of the wool trade and the Ramsden fortune increased.

In about 1770 Sir John, 4th Baronet, embarked on a major remodelling of the old house to the designs of John Carr. The level of the courtyard to the front was raised and although the Ramsden arms over the front door were retained from the earlier house, every effort was made to give Byram the look of a fashionable classical mansion. In particular, a large new 17 bay south wing was added.

Robert Adam was employed to work on parts of the interior in about 1780 and his Library was undoubtedly the best room in the house.

The park was laid out by Capability Brown in 1782 and the pleasure gardens were a nineteenth century triumph.

In the late nineteenth century the Ramsdens moved their principal seat to Bulstrode Park in Buckinghamshire and Byram declined in importance. In 1922 the family sold the mansion and in the 1930's the central section collapsed, although it was not demolished until about 1955.

Byram Park Entrance Front (J. Davidson)

Byram Park Adam Library

FRYSTON HALL,
Castleford

The old house of the Crowles, merchants of Hull, was sold to Richard Slater Milnes in 1788. It was probably he who added the bold classical front, subsequently rebuilt following a fire in 1876.

The Milnes, eventually created Earls of Crewe, entertained Disraeli and other nineteenth century notables at Fryston.

Just before the First World War it was bought for use as a mental asylum but was never used as such. In 1931 the house was dismantled to enjoy an afterlife as building materials for the new Church of the Holy Cross in nearby Airedale. The site is now effectively part of the Ferrybridge Power Station complex.

Fryston Hall (RCHME)

PONTEFRACT NEW HALL

Robert Smythson, architect of Hardwick Hall, Derbyshire, is believed to have designed Pontefract for Edward Talbot, later 8th Earl of Shrewsbury, around 1591. Talbot was Bess of Hardwick's stepson.

Pontefract was a symmetrical building, a constricted centre, with full-height bay window, and spacious wings, beyond which square towers rose. John Carter sketched Pontefract Hall, already abandoned and ruinous, in the early 18th century. Later, part of it was a farmhouse, and by 1897 the railway station had been built close by at Monkhill.

Yet still the ruins survived, and were demolished with dynamite in 1965, the stone being used in the foundations of Wentbridge Viaduct.

Pontefract New Hall, 1885

METHLEY HALL

The departure of the Earls of Mexborough from their family seat at Methley, near Wakefield in many ways symbolised the plight of the landed families in this part of the West Riding. In 1588 their forebear Sir John Savile had bought the fifteenth century house of the Watertons, which he largely rebuilt. He started the work in about 1590 and the architects were almost certainly John and Abraham Akroyd. His son, Sir Henry Savile, had completed it by 1612. The Great Hall was the most important room and contained an elaborately carved Hall Screen dated 1612. There was also an exceptionally good staircase. A Long Gallery had four ten-light windows with painted glass depicting Yorkshire armorials.

Some time before 1778 John, 1st Earl of Mexborough, commissioned John Carr to rebuild the whole suite of rooms along the south-east front, transforming the earlier house in a strictly Palladian manner. Neale describes these rooms as "much better finished, in respect of the decoration of the interior, than most of its size in the kingdom". Pevsner, writing in the 1950's, describes the high rooms with their fine plasterwork in decay.

Anthony Salvin, the darling of the early nineteenth century Yorkshire gentry, was commissioned to carry out further

(1) Methley Hall Entrance Front (J. Davidson)

(2) Methley Hall, hall screen (The Country Life Picture Library)

alterations to the house in 1830-36. Although it was only some fifty years since Carr had remodelled the principal front, his work was completely obliterated by Salvin, acting on behalf of the 3rd Earl of Mexborough. The style was a heavy and rather unconvincing Elizabethan, which may have been more in keeping with the date of the remaining original structure but which, with its twin towers, completely took over the whole composition.

Methley was described in great detail in a Country Life article of 1907, which even then made uncomplimentary remarks about the effects of mining and industry on the surrounding area. The house became simply too good for where it was and was abandoned. A long period of dereliction was ended by its demolition in 1963.

(3) Methley Hall Principal Front by Carr (J. P. Neale).

(4) Methley Hall Principal front as remodelled by Salvin (RCHME)

BISCHOFF HOUSE
(SHEEPSCAR HALL)
Leeds

Nathaniel Denison's house in North Street is shown on Cossins' map of Leeds in 1725. It might have stood a better chance of survival if it had not had the luxury of a front garden, which afforded the opportunity to build a parade of shops onto its distinguished façade. With its Gibbs surrounds to the ground floor windows and an interior of considerable quality, it was possibly the work of William Etty.

The house was previously known as Sheepscar Hall but ended its days as Arthur English's electrical showroom. It was demolished in 1968.

Bischoff House (RCHME)

ROBERT DENISON'S HOUSE,
Leeds

One of the great merchants houses of Leeds, this house in Town End dated from the early eighteenth century and, as Linstrum points out, the entrance doorway and central first floor window are direct copies from the pages of Domenico de Rossi's *Studio d'Architettura Civile*, published in Rome in 1702.

All this suggests that the architect of Denison's house may have been William Thornton, who seems certain to have used the book in the building of Beningbrough, (begun in 1716) for John Bourchier.

This photograph shows the house in about 1880.

Robert Denison's House (R. Hayhurst).

26

POTTERNEWTON HALL,
Leeds

The house was built by the Earls of Mexborough on the site of the Mauleverer's old seat. In October 1935 York antique dealers W.F. Greenwood and Sons offered for sale an "old pine panelled room from the Georgian Mansion Potternewton Hall *Circa 1720*". It was bought and reassembled as the morning room at Sutton Park near York and has been attributed by the owner to Henry Flitcroft (1697-1769), one of Lord Burlington's proteges. If Greenwoods' date is correct it would have been one of his earliest works.

It was demolished to make way for the building of Riviera Gardens.

Potternewton Hall (RCHME).

KILLINGBECK HALL,
Leeds

As late as the 1860's the old hall of the Brookes stood in the grounds of Killingbeck Hall as a ruin. Its successor was said to be of the early eighteenth century and in 1788 William Brooke sold it to the Hansons of Osmondthorpe.

Pevsner described it as "minor", which seems a little unfair despite its rather sorry appearance in its latter years.

In 1898, after having been unoccupied for seventeen years, it was sold to Leeds Corporation for £21,000 to become part of Killingbeck Hospital and was demolished in 1978.

Killingbeck Hall (Leeds City Libraries).

KNOWSTHORPE HOUSE,
Leeds

Sometimes referred to as Knostrop New Hall, this was a handsome country house built by Abraham Rhodes on his estate in what was then the rural Aire valley. The entrance front was fairly plain but the garden front, likened to a Wyatt composition, was more interesting, with a two-storey bay into which the saloon projected. The wings had a matching pair of pavilions. Internal photographs show a good staircase behind a screen of two columns.

In the later nineteenth century it was the property of the Leather family.

It was demolished in about 1962.

Knowsthorpe House (Leeds City Libraries).

ALWOODLEY OLD HALL,
Leeds

This sad photograph was taken in 1966, three years before the house finally disappeared and after a long period of dereliction. Pevsner noted its rare stepped gable windows.

Its status was usurped when the new hall was built in 1825 but prior to that Alwoodley had long been the seat of the Franks.

In 1630 the manor was bought by Sir Gervase Clifton and the estate changed hands again in 1661, this time to Cornelius Clarke. The first Lord Bingley bought it in 1729 and it passed through marriage to the Lane Fox family, in whose possession it remained.

Alwoodley Old House (RCHME)

HORSFORTH HALL

Horsforth Hall was started by John Stanhope in 1699 and completed in 1707. Buck's sketch of about 1720 shows its pleasing lines, which lost something of their simplicity when it was altered for another John Stanhope by John Watson (d. 1771) in 1767.

The heavy pediment and classical door surround were probably added (and the dormers removed) at this time.

In 1930 the Yorkshire Weekly Post reported that Horsforth Hall had been purchased by an anonymous person and given to the town. This attempt to save the building was in vain and it was demolished in the early 1950's.

Horsforth Hall (Contemporary Biographies).

LOWER HALL, Liversedge

This was one of the larger seventeenth manor houses in the area, which ended its days split into tenements, like so many of its contemporaries.

It was built in about 1660 by William Greene, nephew of Lieut. Greene, the owner of Liversedge Hall, funded by the proceeds of the cloth trade.

Typically West Riding, its stone exterior was finally covered with render and the leaded lights were replaced with plate glass. Despite this, there were still some interesting fireplaces in the house when Louis Ambler described it in 1913.

An estate of 1960's houses now stands in the grounds and all that remains of the hall itself is a stable and a wall with the sign "Lower Hall" attached.

Lower Hall, Liversdge (R. Hayhurst)

BARDEN TOWER,
Barden-in-Wharfedale

The ruins of Barden Tower, an early 16th century tower house, stand slightly away from the still-occupied cottage, chapel and lower tower. Of three storeys, with late Gothic details, Barden was built for Lord Clifford, and restored by Lady Anne Clifford in 1658-59.

In 1900 the lower tower and cottage were in use as a farmhouse, and services were still held in the chapel, conducted by the Rector of Bolton Priory.

LEFT: Barden Tower (J. Davidson)   *ABOVE: Plate from Whitaker's Craven*

SUTTON HALL,
Sutton-in-Craven

Sutton Hall stood for 47 years. It was a somewhat grim Renaissance-style building designed by Samuel Jackson in 1893 for John Hartley, worsted manufacturer at Greenroyd Mill.

In 1933 it was sold to E. Turner, a Keighley builder. For a time, five families lived there. Sutton Hall was demolished c.1940 and some of the stone was used as foundations for the houses and bungalows built on the site.

Sutton Hall

MILNER FIELD, Saltaire

Near his model industrial village of Saltaire, Titus Salt built Milner Field in 1871-73 to a design by Thomas Harris, possibly advised by Richard Norman Shaw. The style was described by *Building News* as "twelfth century medieval", an assemblage of circular conical-capped towers, great chimney stacks and machicolations, all raised up on a terrace. The service wing led to an octagonal kitchen recalling Glastonbury. Interior carving was by Thomas Nicholls, glass was by Saunders & Co., and paintings were by Fred Weeks. Salt designed his own elaborate set of conservatories. It was in ruins by the 1950's.

Milner Field (The Builder, 15th March 1873)

THE KNOLL, Baildon

Built by Charles Stead in 1858 in Victorian Gothic style. Its tower and higher turret, and the bell-cote on the gable end gave it a slightly ecclesiastical or monastic appearance. Sir James Roberts was a later owner. He eventually moved to Milner Field. The local council bought The Knoll in 1946. For some time it was divided into flats but was later demolished.

The Knoll, Baildon (Bradford Telegraph & Argus)

ST. IVES,
Bingley

Benjamin Ferrand's father moved to St. Ives in 1712 from nearby Harden Grange. James Paine designed a new house for Benjamin Ferrand in 1759. A three-bay central section of three storeys with a pediment roof, was flanked by two-storey, two-bay wings with hipped roofs. A service block was built directly behind the house and connected by a short corridor. In 1854 the Ferrand family returned to their older seat and called it St. Ives, the Paine house became Harden Grange, but the main building was demolished in 1859. The service wing became the core of the present building.

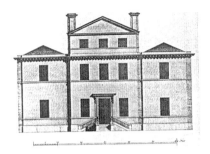

St. Ives (James Paine, Noblemen and gentlemen's houses, vol.1, 1767)

GREENHOLME VILLA,
Burley-in-Wharfedale

William Foster and William Fison bought Greenholme Mills and estate in 1850. They converted the old cotton mills to worsted manufacturing.

Fison lived at Greenholme Villa, the old home of the Whitakers, rebuilt 1820 in neo-classical style. Fison's son Frederick W. Fison owned it after his father. By the early 20th century Greenholme was let, and after the 1914-18 war the old lifestyle was impossible to maintain.

The Villa was demolished in 1922-23, the stone being used to build houses on Great Pasture. No satisfactory picture of Greenholme in its prime has been found.

Greenholme Villa in demolition

HAYFIELD,
Glusburn

A modest villa for worsted spinner James Hartley, Hayfield was acquired by his partner John Cousen Horsfall in the 1870s and massively extended. The work, in the Italianate style, was a picturesque grouping of extensions, bay windows and arcades, around a central pyramid-roofed tower. John Kirk of Huddersfield has been suggested as the architect. In 1922 it was the home of Sir John Donald, Bart.

Hayfield (W.H. Scott, The West Riding at the opening of the 20th century, 1902)

NEWALL OLD HALL,
near Otley

By the mid-19th century Newall Old Hall had become a farmhouse. The core of the house is thought to have been a medieval pele-tower, but considerable additions were made in the 17th century and later. The east and west wings were reconstructed in 1827. The illustration is thought to be somewhat fanciful. Newall was demolished in 1928. A housing estate for Otley Council covers the site.

Newall Old Hall (R. Hayhurst)

OAKWORTH HOUSE, Keighley

Sir Isaac Holden (1807-97) had the world's largest wool-carding business in Bradford and France. His second wife preferred Yorkshire to France, and in 1864-74 Holden transformed her modest house to designs by Bradford architect George Smith. Behind the house was a vast complex of hothouses including a 2-acre winter garden. Two huge furnaces, the chimneys of which rose like Italian campanili, heated the water for the house. By the 1880's the house was lit by home-generated electricity. The house had a hydrant system as a fire precaution, but burnt down in 1909. The site was given to Oakworth by Francis Illingworth in 1925 as a public park.

Oakworth House (Picturesque views of castles and country houses in Yorkshire, 1885)

STRONG CLOSE HOUSE, Keighley

A somewhat French-inspired house begun in 1864 for Keighley mill-owner Joseph Craven, perhaps by the architect Samuel Jackson. Craven's mill was close by, and in order to gain a belvedere to view his landscape, Craven had a campanile built round the mill chimney, with a staircase rising to a platform near the top. Strong Close House did not long survive Craven and his widow, and was demolished in 1910.

Strong Close House (R. Hayhurst)

LITTLEMOOR, Queensbury

At Queensbury in Wharfedale were several mansions for 19th century West Riding industrialists. Littlemoor was a huge house in the Scottish baronial style for Herbert Anderson Foster (1853-1930). He was a partner in Black Dyke Mills. After his death Littlemoor was empty, and in 1953 his widow Edith Foster gave the estate to the local council, to be used as a park. Littlemoor, in poor condition, was demolished.

LEFT: Littlemoor (R. Hayhurst)   *ABOVE: Littlemoor (J. Davidson)*

HARROWINS, Queensbury

A more conventional house in the Victorian Tudor style, Harrowins was built c.1850 by William Foster (1821-84), manging director of Foster's Mill. It had an impressive array of conservatories including one in the Gothic style. Foster inherited Hornby Castle, Lancashire, in 1878.

His second son Robert Foster (1850-1925) inherited Harrowins from his father, but later acquired Stockeld Park near Wetherby and went to live there.

Harrowins (R. Hayhurst)

BIERLEY HALL,
Bradford

The seat of the Richardson family was drawn by Samuel Buck c.1720. It was dated 1636, a centre and two wings. The centre was remodelled later in the 17th century, with new windows, a door with a scrolled pediment, and elaborate round-headed gables, each pierced with an oculus and capped with urns. A further remodelling of c.1750 for Richard Richardson was probably by James Paine. There were new windows, and a porch, and the gabling was replaced by a heavy attic with a giant pediment pierced by a lunette window. The staircase hall had a rococo ceiling with emblems of architecture, sculpture, painting and music. In the gardens were 18th century picturesque features - lakes, a grotto and a druids' circle. Near the hall was a Cedar of Lebanon, presented to Dr. Richardson by his friend Sir Hans Sloane. Richardson had the second hot-house to be built in England. In the 19th century Bierley was owned by Miss Currer of Eshton Hall. About 1800 the Bierley Iron Works started nearby, with coal and ironstone drawn from the estate. The Hall was tenanted. By 1897 Bierley had been bought by Bradford Corporation for a hospital for infectious diseases. Later it was an old people's hospital. It was finally replaced by a modern hospital building in 1968, and demolished soon after.

(1) Bierley Hall c.1720, after Samuel Buck

(2) Bierley Hall (Bradford Metropolitan City Council)

BRADFORD MANOR HOUSE

The manor house of the Rawson family was built in the early 16th century. It was rebuilt in 1705 for William Rawson, and drawn c.1720 by Samuel Buck. It was a double-pile house, of brick with stone dressings, three storeys and a basement, with baroque decoration of the main entrance and the window above. The stair-hall had mural paintings by Parmentier, who did much work in Yorkshire. On the walls were reliefs of Perseus and Andromeda, and Bacchus and Ariadne. The ceiling depicted the four seasons. The Rawsons made a fortune in iron-working, and Benjamin Rawson eventually bought Nidd Hall near Harrogate. In 1824 the precincts began to be used as a market, and the house was empty. It was demolished in the early 1860s. The Market Buildings in Kirkgate stand on the site.

(1) Bradford Manor House (William Scruton, Pen and pencil sketches of old Bradford, 1899)

(2) Bradford Manor House, c.1860

HEATON HALL,
Bradford

The seat of the Fields from the 16th century. John Field rebuilt Heaton after 1660, but it was remodelled in Palladian style c.1750. After John Wilmer Field died in 1837 Heaton passed to the Earl of Rosse (1800-67) of Birr Castle, Ireland. His widow lived much at Heaton until she died in 1885. The rooms had elaborate mid-18th century decoration, plaster ceilings and marble chimneypieces. Some 17th century rooms remained, including one panelled in black oak. Heaton was later tenanted, mostly by Bradford businessmen. The estate was sold in 1911, and semi-detached houses were built. The Hall was demolished before 1939. A school occupies the site.

(1) Heaton Hall (Bradford Metropolitan City Council)

(2) Heaton Hall, side wing (J.S. King)

(3) Heaton Hall, fireplace (W. Cudworth, History of Manningham ... 1896)

MANNINGHAM HALL,
Bradford

Manningham Hall was demolished about 1900 and the Cartwright Hall Art Gallery, a swaggering Baroque building opened in 1904, stands on its site. Manningham, the seat of the Lister family, was built c.1770 on the site of the old hall. It was brick with stone dressings. S.C. Lister, later Lord Masham, built a factory on the hill above. He left Manningham for Farfield Hall, and sold the Hall and park to Bradford Council in 1870. For a while the Hall was used as a restaurant (with the word 'Refreshments' affixed to the parapet).

Manningham Hall (W. Cudworth, History of Manningham ... 1896)

WOODLANDS,
Girlington

The residence of Angus Holden, Mayor of Bradford, later 1st Lord Alston. About two miles from Bradford, Woodlands was designed by Milner and France about 1865. It was a powerful Gothic composition, with a tall tower at the centre of the entrance front. The turret was an observatory. At the centre of the house was a two-storey hall, with glazed roof, in which hung Holden's extensive picture collection. The staircase winding round the hall had metal panels by Skidmore, the famous Coventry metal-worker. A music room was afterwards added with an apsidal window containing stained glass by Burne-Jones.

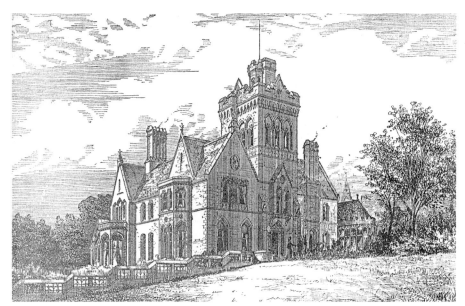

Woodlands (Picturesque views of castles and country houses in Yorkshire, 1885)

HORTON HALL,
Bradford

The Sharp family had two houses on Little Horton Green, of which Horton Hall was the grander. The old part of the Hall was rebuilt c.1677 by Thomas Sharp. It incorporated a late medieval timber-framed building, and some of the rooms had oak panelling and decorated ceilings. The porch of the rebuilt Hall bore the date 1677. The old Hall was originally symmetrical, a centre and two wings, the wings with 'Dutch' gables, and all the windows with mullions and transoms. The astronomer Abraham Sharp (1651-1742), assistant to Flamsteed and friend of Sir Isaac Newton, lived at Horton Hall and in 1694 raised the central porch to make a flat-topped, balustraded tower, for use as his observation post. The tower incorporated a rose window, a common feature of houses in that area at that period. In c.1800 one wing was demolished and a new block, plain classical, with canted bay windows, was built. It was somewhat in the style of John Carr. Horton was once the home of Edward Hailstone, well-known antiquary and Yorkshire topographer. In 1902 J. Cawthra lived at Horton. The Hall fell into decay in the 1950's. There was a serious fire in 1965, and Horton was demolished soon after.

(1) Horton Hall (W.H. Scott, the West Riding ... at the opening of the 20th century, 1902)

(2) Horton Hall, 17th century wing

HORTON OLD HALL,
Bradford

The other Sharp family house on Little
Horton Green was Horton Old Hall,
built in 1675 by Isaac Sharp. It was a
traditional design, a recessed centre and
two large wings, with large mullioned
and transomed windows. The round
headed doorway led to a porch and the
main hall in the centre of the building, a
fine oak-panelled room with a gallery at
the end. Francis Sharp Powell, last
owner of the estate, lived here. Horton
Old Hall was demolished c.1966.

Horton Old Hall

ALLERTON HALL,
Bradford

A small house of 1785 for Joshua Firth,
brick with stone quoins, a small pediment
over the entrance bay. Later it was
owned by Benjamin Kaye, master clothier,
who organised home-weavers and took
their wares weekly to Manchester. In the
late 19th century Sir F.S. Powell was the
owner. Allerton fell into disrepair and
was purchased by Bradford Council and
demolished in 1968.

Allerton Hall

41

SHELF HALL,
near Bradford

Big and boldly baroque, with its
Corinthian pedimented portico and its
corner pavilions capped with balustrades
and urns, Shelf Hall was not at all a
fashionable style for 1861. The patron
was Samuel Bottomley (1819-83),
worsted manufacturer, the architect was
perhaps J.T. Fairbank of Bradford. The
cost was over £40,000. The estate covered
27 acres, and included 'a glen unsurpassed
for beauty'. It was owned by Bottomley's
eldest son Nathaniel (who changed his
surname to Cautley).

In the 1914-18 War it was a prisoner-
of-war camp. Afterwards it was bought
by the local council and demolished.

Shelf Hall (Bradford Telegraph & Argus)

TINGLEY HALL,
Morley

A mid-18th century house on the highest
ground in West Ardsley township. By
the mid-19th century the hall and estate
were owned by the proprietor of
Topcliffe pit. In 1897 Henry Longbottom
lived there and in the 1920s Alderman
Brown Fraser, who organised music
festivals at the Hall. It was a house for
Italian prisoners in the 1939-45 War.

Afterwards it was converted into
four flats. Tingley was demolished in
1967 for a new dual carriageway from
Dewsbury.

Tingley Hall (D.K. Atkinson)

HATFEILD HALL,
Stanley

The 17th century seat of the Hatfeild family was built on the site of Woodhall by Gervase Hatfeild (d.1654). There were dates 1598 and 1608 on shields, which perhaps reflected the start and finish of the rebuilding. John Hatfeild (1698-1764) remodelled the house in 18th century Gothick style, perhaps c.1750. A print of 1780 shows Hatfeild in its Gothick dress, with pointed windows on the ground floor and sashes above, and battlements throughout, the gables decorated with slim, elongated pinnacles. These were later removed, but recent photographs show a still substantial Gothick character. Hatfeild's son, John Hatfeild Kaye was a considerable antiquary and amassed 60 folio volumes of notes for a history of Yorkshire, now all dispersed. In 1897 James Hatfeild Harter sold the house (which had been let to tenants) to Herbert Beaumont, solictor, of Wakefield. His son Gerald Beaumont sold Hatfeild to the West Riding County Council in 1921 for use as a hospital. It is now a ruin and the estate covered in pit-workings.

(1) Hatfield Hall (Angus Taylor)

(2) Hatfield Hall (Angus Taylor)

HEATH OLD HALL,
Heath

Heath village had three big houses around its large common: James Paine's Heath House, John Carr's Heath Hall, and Heath Old Hall, demolished in 1961 following mining subsidence. It was built c.1585-90 and because of its similarity to Robert Smythson's Barlborough Hall, Derbyshire, Heath has been attributed to Smythson also. The builder was John Kaye, deputy steward of the Honour of Pontefract. It was a square house with four polygonal corner turrets, of three storeys with an intricate pierced parapet. A great flight of steps swept up to the front door. A long gallery ran along the front at first floor level, and behind it was the great hall. A first-floor room had a large fireplace carved with pairs of columns, Ionic below, Corinthian above, and a carved overmantel frieze of Jezebel. Another room had 18th century Gothick decoration. The Hall and its history were fully recorded in 1889 by Lady Green in *The Old Hall at Heath*. Lady Green was a later occupant. Mark Girouard, who saw Heath in its last years, wrote 'the decay and ruination of the house, the industrial landscape, the huge cooling-towers next door, gave it a tremendous poignancy.'

(1) Heath Old Hall (R. Hayhurst)

(2) Heath Old Hall, by W. Coney (Gott collection, Wakefield Art Gallery)

44

MORLEY HOUSE

Morley House, a large three-storey Georgian house with standard Palladian features, a first-floor Venetian window and a lunette above, was the home of the Scatcherd family for over two centuries. Norrisson Cavendish Scatcherd wrote a *History of Morley* in 1830. Later it was the home of R. Borrough Hopkins, who left the site as an extension to Scatcherd Park in 1936. Morley House was demolished about this time.

Morley House (D.K. Atkinson)

HAGUE HALL,
South Kirkby

A 17th century gabled house of three storeys, the windows later Georgianised. Hague passed through several families until from the mid-18th century it was in the hands of the Allotts. When Kelly's published their 1897 *Directory,* Hague Hall was unoccupied.

Hague Hall (R. Hayhurst)

BLAKE HALL,
Mirfield

Close to Mirfield church, Blake Hall was owned by the Turners in the 18th century and the Inghams in the 19th century. William Turner rebuilt the Hall in classical style in 1747, and Joshua Ingham (d.1866) made additions in 1845, including a staircase and bay window, to designs by Ignatius Bonomi of Durham. Anne Bronte was governess to Ingham's children in 1839, and wrote about her experiences in *Agnes Grey* (as Wellwood House and the Bloomfields). The Ingham fortunes were sustained by nearby Thornhill Colliery, but after 1918 it began to fail, and Mirfield was growing rapidly. Major Joshua Ingham moved out in 1921, eventually settling at Wighill Hall. The new owners, Blake Hall Estate Ltd., sold the park for building plots, and the senior director of the company, Maurice Avison, occupied the Hall 1931-51. It was afterwards empty and was demolished in 1954 for its fittings and materials. The Blake Hall housing estate now occupies the site.

(1) Blake Hall (R. Hayhurst)

(2) Blake Hall (B. Tattersfield)

HOWLEY HALL,
near Morley

Demolished in 1730, Howley is illustrated in Whitaker's *Leodis and Elmet,* from a lost painting by John Settrington. It was a vast Elizabethan house with corner towers and little cupolas, built by Sir John Savile, of the Methley family, at the same time as Methley, c.1590, but on a grander scale. The courtyard was 60 yards square. The entrance porch had two orders of twin columns: a gatehouse replicated it. Lord Cardigan ordered its demolition. Much stone was used in houses in Morley and Batley, and panelling in houses and a chapel in Wakefield and Bradford.

Howley Hall (18th century engraving of a painting attributed to John Settrington)

NEWLAND HALL, Normanton

Newland Hall stood on the site of a Knights Hospitallers preceptory, an order dissolved in 1540. The estate passed through several families' hands. In the 18th century John Smith (d.1746) was the owner, and afterwards his son Sir John Silvester Smith (1744-89). In the time of his grandson, Sir Matthew Dodsworth (d.1858), Newland was sold to William Locke for £35,000. The Hall, a good classical composition of five bays, with a central entrance *in antis,* a pedimented tripartite window above and a lunette window on the second floor, was presumably rebuilt by John Smith, since the surviving stables are dated 1745. Newland was demolished in 1920.

Newland Hall (John Goodchild)

JOHN MILNE'S HOUSE,
Wakefield

Built in 1773 for John Milnes, it was a five-bay, three-storey rectangular house (cf. Campsmount), and extended in the 1790's with quadrant wings. There was a suite of rooms, library, drawing room and ballroom (the fine ceilings in this part of the house were painted by Italian artists). The house had extensive gardens. In 1856 the Wakefield - Leeds railway line was built close by, and part of the house became the station. The house was demolished in the 1960's for use as a youth centre.

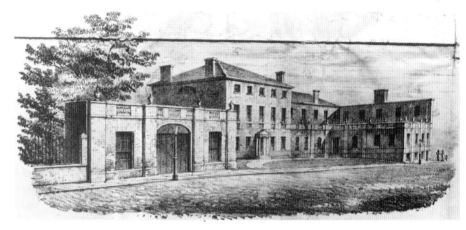

John Milnes' house (John Goodchild)

THORNES HOUSE,
Wakefield

John Carr designed Thornes in 1779 for James Milnes, a cloth merchant, on an elevated site outside Wakefield. It was of five bays and three storeys (like John Milnes' house) the entrance front being of stone, with a pediment and fluted Ionic pilasters, the rest brick, with a canted bay window on the garden front. The rooms were Adamesque, delicately detailed and coloured. Milnes was succeeded by his great nephew Benjamin Gaskell, and it remained a Gaskell residence until 1919, when it was sold to Wakefield Corporation, and converted into a secondary school. It was burnt in 1951 and demolished.

Thornes House (E. Yates)

ALVERTHORP HALL, Wakefield

The Maudes were at Alverthorp from the early 17th century. The Hall was rebuilt for Daniel Maude around 1700. It had seven bays, with quoined corners and a parapet, partly balustraded, and a segmental-headed porch with stone pilasters above. In 1764 Alverthorp was bought by Sir Thomas Lowther of Swillington, whose second son John moved to Swillington Hall in 1798. Wakefield solicitor Benjamin Clarkson bought Alverthorp in 1800. Sisters Louisa and Christabel Clarkson were the last residents, until the mid-20th century, 'whose artistic skill was displayed in the decoration of the interior of the house and in the development of the gardens'.

Alverthorpe Hall (John Goodchild)

OUTWOOD HALL and SPRINGFIELD HOUSE, Wakefield

Several villas on the outskirts of Wakefield are now demolished.

Outwood was a plain 18th century house rudely medievalised in the 19th century by the addition of battlements and a stepped-gable wing leading to an octagonal tower. Springfield had a medieval touch, with battlements, contrasting oddly with its pedimented porch and Regency bow windows.

Outwood Hall (John Goodchild)

Springfield House (John Goodchild)

CHEVET HALL,
near Wakefield

The architectural history of Chevet has not been fully elucidated. It was a seemingly 18th century and early 19th century house, but this concealed a prehistory as a large early Tudor mansion. Sir John Nevile (d.1541) married Elizabeth, heiress of the previous owners, the Bosviles. A beam in the house recorded 'This Hows was mad by John Nevyll, knight, and dame Elizabeth hys wyfe... 1529', and a building account survives in the Chevet deeds, mentioning a great hall, great chamber, several other chambers, great and little galleries, chapel, kitchen, brewhouse and gatehouse. After the death of John Nevile in 1720, Chevet passed to the representative of another branch, the Revd. Cavendish Neville, Vicar of Norton, who started the process of rebuilding and enlargement and added the Palladian south front. He died in 1749 and Chevet passed to the Pilkington family. Several generations of Pilkingtons were at Chevet, and Sir Thomas Pilkington (1773-1811) employed his uncle the architect John Rawsthorne to make alterations, including a new stairhall with a Greek Revival screen. In Sir Lionel Pilkington's time (1835-1901), Chevet was encased in stone,

(1) Chevet Hall, south-east front (RCHME)

(2) Chevet Hall, south-west front (RCHME)

having been either rough-hewn stone plastered, or else entirely 'pebble-dashed'. Sir Thomas Milborne-Swinnerton-Pilkington was the owner until the 1939-45 War. Afterwards it was disused and was demolished in 1955.

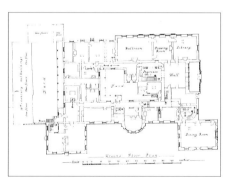

(3) Chevet Hall, north-west front (RCHME)

(4) Chevet Hall, principal stair hall (RCHME)

(5) Chevet Hall, ground floor plan (RCHME)

WHITLEY BEAUMONT, Kirkheaton

The Beaumonts lived at Whitley Beaumont from the 13th century. The hall was rebuilt about 1560 with a great hall flanked by two wings forming a courtyard. In 1680 Richard Beaumont obtained plans from Thomas Mann of York for a new range to close the courtyard. This was not begun until 1704. The new front of the house was sturdy and baroque, with a centrepiece of a pedimented doorcase with a window above with scrolled decoration of the frame, all enclosed in giant pilasters and a segmental pediment. The inner face of the new range had a stone arcade connecting the rooms around the courtyard. James Paine remodelled the great hall for his brother-in-law Richard Beaumont in rococo style c.1752-54. He probably designed garden buildings also, including the now ruinous gazebo or summer house on a hill near the house. Capability Brown probably landscaped the grounds in the 1760's and 1780's.

Whitley Beaumont's fittings were sold at auction in 1917. Charles E. Sutcliffe bought the house in 1924, but did not live there regularly. It gradually fell into disrepair. T. Reginald Sutcliffe inherited it but sold it in 1950 to

(1) Whitley Beaumont

(2) Whitley Beaumont, saloon (J. Barnes-Gorell)

Bradford & Leeds Properties Syndicate who split up the estate. The hall was bought for £2,500 by James Warne of Warnegate Products, Halifax, with the intention of demolishing it. Demolition began late in 1950. The Park had been requisitioned by the Ministry of Fuel in 1947 for open-cast coal mining.

(3) Whitley Beaumont, dining saloon (A. Broadbent)

DENBY GRANGE, Flockton

Arthur Kaye bought the estate in the sixteenth century and his successors had extended the house by 1636. An early nineteenth century print shows a gabled wing. The new mansion was probably built by Sir John Lister Kaye (1725-89) although both date and architect are unknown. Another Sir John (1801-71) faced financial pressures and let it to Julius Silberman in 1843 but he became insolvent.

In 1948 Sir Kenneth Lister Kaye bought an estate in Ireland, sold the contents and abandoned Denby Grange. Job Earnshaw & Bros Ltd, timber merchants, bought the house and 1039 acres in 1949. It was demolished in 1950.

Denby Grange (John Goodchild)

PYE NEST,
Halifax

Pye Nest was not the first house to occupy this site in the Skircoat area but it was John Edwards' house of 1767 that crumbled under the contractor's hammer in 1935. The rich Halifax merchant chose John Carr, the most eminent Yorkshire architect of his day, and the end result with its Palladian lines including quadrants and pavilions must have been the envy of his neighbours. So much so that William Walker commissioned Thomas Bradley to reproduce it at nearby Crow Nest (q.v.) a few years later.

One of the most distinguished Halifax houses of its era, it passed to Sir Henry Edwards, whose death in 1886 prompted Messrs Walton and Lee to offer it for sale on 3rd August 1887. The sale catalogue gives a detailed description of the interior, with a special mention of the entrance hall which was lit from a central dome above. At that time it still had 134 acres but failed to find a buyer. It finally passed out of the family's hands on 22nd July 1932 when the executors of the late Major A.H. Edwards sold it with 23 acres. The site was developed for housing.

(1) Pye Nest (RCHME)

(2) Pye Nest 1935 (Halifax Central Library)

CROW NEST, Halifax

Rarely can there have been such a blatant example of architectural plagiarism as occurred at Crow Nest in 1778. William Walker, a manufacturer of worsted goods, demolished the old house of the Mitchells and commissioned Thomas Bradley to copy John Carr's nearby Pye Nest of 1767. Bradley's only other recorded work was an unexecuted design for the Halifax Piece Hall.

In 1775 Walker had taken the remarkable step of chartering a vessel from Hull and travelling to the Baltic to purchase a cargo of timber to be used for the building of (among other properties) Crow Nest. This was then shipped to Brighouse by the Aire and Calder Navgation Company before coming to Crow Nest on wagons.

Not surprisingly, given its provenance, Crow Nest was an accomplished design. It stood in an 82 acre park; in 1861 the carriage drive was constructed and a triumphal arch created. Sir Titus Salt, millowner and philanthropist, had rented the house from 1844 to 1858 and bought it privately after an abortive auction in 1867. Sir Titus's momentous 50th birthday celebrations of 1856 were themselves eclipsed by a monster party in 1873, to which 4200 guests were invited.

In 1878 his executors sold to another mill-owner, Richard Kershaw. Partying continued and the six day sale following his death in 1917 included some 500 bottles of vintage port. It was never again occupied as a private house and lay in ruins by the 1950's. The nineteenth century lodge remains.

Crow Nest (G. Kershaw)

Crow Nest, The West Wing 1917 (G. Kershaw)

HIGH SUNDERLAND,
Halifax

This was one of the West Riding's great seventeenth century houses, a gaunt battlemented mansion of 1629 that stood on moorland outside Halifax. It is believed to have incorporated an earlier half-timbered mediaeval house.

The builder was Abraham Sunderland and his aim was to impress. Large extravagantly carved figures stood over the entrance and on the banqueting house; an inscription pleaded that the family should be allowed to "quietly inhabit this seat ... until an ant drink up the waters of the sea, and a tortoise walk round the whole world".

Sadly, this was not to be and by the twentieth century it had been divided into tenements. Mining was blamed for the bulging walls but a report by the Ministry of Works in 1947 expressed the opinion that it could be saved if £6,000 could be found.

By then it was in a ruinous condition and its demolition in 1950 was probably inevitable. Prior to that it had become something of a local cause celebre with attempts being made to retain the façade, in vain. Parts of the building were removed with a view to their re-erection at a local businessman's home in Lightcliffe. Other parts, including decorative stonework and a gateway are in the possession of Bankfield Museum.

(1) High Sunderland Main Front (C. Wells).

(2) High Sunderland Entrance (C. Wells).

MANOR HEATH, Halifax

The Crossley family's contribution to Halifax was immense, so it was particularly sad that it was the local authority that demolished John Crossley's mansion in 1958. His fabulous wealth had been made from the industrial production of carpets at Dean Clough.

Six architects competed for the commission, which was won by Parnell and Smith, whose designs are dated 1852-3. Heavily gothic, it was all gables and chimneys. Social acceptability was assured when the Prince of Wales stayed the night in 1863.

In 1929 it was bought by Halifax Corporation for £18,500. It was replaced it with a rose garden.

Manor Heath (Halifax Courier)

WELL HEAD HOUSE, Halifax

The fact that Well Head House and its 20 acre park just a few hundred yards from the centre of Halifax, survived intact into the late twentieth century was a miracle in itself. The prevarication of the local council that led to its destruction was a tragedy.

A handsome classical villa that appears to have been built for John and Elizabeth Waterhouse following their wedding in 1767, it remained in the family's ownership until 1916. It was vacated by the Lees family in 1968 but continuous changes of heart by the council left it a vandalised shell and it was demolished in 1976 to make way for housing.

Well Head House (RCHME)

CASTLE CARR, Luddenden Dean

"A noble and stately pile of buildings" said the sale particulars of 1874. "Unloveably grim" commented Linstrum. This huge house was built for Leah Priestley Edwards, son of Sir Henry Edwards of Pye Nest (q.v.) in 1859-72, to the designs first of Thomas Risling, then of John Hogg. The grand hall was sixty feet high and the style an unusual blend of Norman and Elizabethan, arranged round a central courtyard.

It failed to sell at auction in 1874 but was sold by Edwards in 1876.

The last owners were the Yorkshire Water Authority who built the Dean Head reservoirs behind it. The house was demolished in 1962.

Castle Carr (Halifax Courier)

CRAGG HALL,
Cragg Vale

There was something rather appealing about Cragg Hall, with its confusion of architectural styles apparently influenced by various European countries. It belonged to the Hinchcliffe family, cotton spinners in the Halifax area.

Enter Algernon Simpson, bank clerk and third husband to the Hinchcliffe heiress, who took the name Simpson-Hinchcliffe and lived the high life at Cragg Hall, owning a racehorse called Broadwood which lent its name to a row of cottages in Cragg Vale.

His bride died in 1917 and Cragg Hall lasted little longer. In 1921 it was gutted in a huge fire.

Cragg Hall (J. Davidson).

58

UPPER SHIBDEN HALL, near Halifax

Standing at the head of Shibden Dean just outside Halifax, the gaunt remains of Upper Shibden Hall are as romantic a ruin as you will find in the West Riding. The burnt out shell with its tower and large bay window still enjoys spectacular views to the south as far, it is said, as the High Peaks. Across the park lies an equally ruinous and roofless lodge.

Originally called Catherine House, after the slack on which it was built, it was the creation of colliery owner and brewer Michael Stocks. It dated from about 1800.

Upper Shibden Hall.

BROOMHEAD HALL, Penistone

Still a substantial ruin, Broomhead Hall stood five miles south of Penistone, with fine views over to Wharncliffe. There had been an earlier house on the site. The gabled mock-Tudor mansion, an early example of this style in Yorkshire, was built in 1831 by James Rimington. Pevsner was particularly impressed by the imposing entrance hall with its glazed ceiling and early Georgian staircase, which came from Kiverton Park, near Rotherham.

The illustrious inhabitants of the earlier hall were the Wilsons. The Rimingtons added the name to their own to produce, among others, the splendidly titled Reginald Henry Rimington Rimington-Wilson, who lived there in 1908.

Broomhead Hall (J. Davidson).

DARRINGTON HALL,
near Pontefract

The 17th century wing of Darrington Hall was demolished in the 1980's; the 19th century section remains, in a housing estate. Darrington was mostly the home of the lord of the manor's steward. The only lord who resided regularly was Samuel Savile (d.1735). He probably put the 17th century wing into its final form. Darrington passed to the Sotheron family and then to Thomas Sotheron-Estcourt. The Sotheron-Estcourts preferred to live on their Gloucestershire estates. In 1919 Lady Katherine Pilkington transformed Darrington into a hospital for ex-servicemen, and the 60-patient hospital was controlled by the Ministry of Pensions.

Darrington Hall, 17th century wing (J.S. Fletcher, Memorials of a Yorkshire parish, 1917)

ELMSALL LODGE,
North Elmsall

Elmsall Lodge was a small mid-eighteenth century villa built for Fane Cholmley. It was of three bays, with canted bay windows on the garden side. After Cholmley's death it was mostly inhabited by tenants. The house has been demolished but the stables survive.

Elmsall Lodge (R. Hayhurst)

60

FEATHERSTONE MANOR,
near Pontefract

Demolished in the early 1960's, Featherstone Manor stood on the main street, a centre and one wing only (was the other wing demolished, or never built?). It was once the residence of the Hippon family, who were hereditary gamekeepers in Pontefract Park until Queen Elizabeth's reign. By 1897 it was in use in use as a farmhouse, and grew dilapidated, and by the early 1960's had come to the end of its useful life.

Featherstone Manor (A.A. Lumb)

ACKTON HALL,
Featherstone

Ackton Hall, an early 17th century house, was bought by Thomas Wynn and enlarged in 1765, with a plain but well-proportioned seven-bay front having a three-bay pediment. Ackton passed to his son Sir Edmund Wynn and to his great nieces, who sold it in 1865 to George Bradley. On bradley's death in 1896 Ackton was sold to T. Middleton of Leeds. He intended to let the Hall and build houses on the estate, but nearby collieries ruined the view. The next owner Mr Lister converted Ackton into fire houses. By 1969 the Hall had become so dilapidated that it was demolished

Ackton Hall (A.A. Lumb)

ACKWORTH PARK

In 1763 Sir Francis Sykes bought the estate from the last collateral representatives of the Lowther family. A drawing in the Gott Collection at Wakefield shows the 17th century house standing on an eminence and with wooded hills behind. The house was remodelled in the late 1760's (by James Paine?). It passed through several hands - Alderman Solly, Mr. Petyt, John Gully (see Cocken Hall in *Lost Houses of County Durham*) and Henry Hill. By 1897 it was in the hands of trustees, and had remained unoccupied for some time. It was described as 'a handsome building of stone', with a conservatory, greenhouse and peach-house. Ackworth was demolished in the 1950s.

(1) Ackworth Park, 17th century house (Gott Collection, Wakefield Art Gallery)

(2) Ackworth Park (J. Davidson)

62

BADSWORTH HALL

Badsworth, the seat of the Brights until the early 18th century, was, after the marriage of a Bright heiress to the Marquess of Rockingham, usually tenanted. It was late 17th century or early 18th century in style, of three storeys, the top storey windows still capped with Tudor-style hood moulds. John Carr of York made alterations for the 2nd Marquess of Rockingham c.1780. For many years it was a sporting seat of the Earl of Darlington (1st Duke of Cleveland, 1833). It was ruinous by 1965, and later demolished. The stables were converted into a house.

Badsworth Hall (Catherine Smith)

EDENTHORPE,
Kirk Sandall

Formerly known as Streetthorpe, the estate was purchased in 1769 by George Cooke, who built the blockish and plain house, similar to Campsmount. In the 1870's the estate was owned by Lord Auckland, who enlarged the house and changed its name to Edenthorpe, his family name being Eden. He sold it in 1897 and by 1908 it was the property of Earl Fitzwilliam. In the 1920's the central part was gutted by fire and demolished. The park was used for building. The north wing became flats, the south wing a house for the then owner, Lord Moncrieff. It was later a school.

Edenthorpe Hall (Doncaster Library)

CAMPSALL HALL

Campsall was the seat of the Frank family from the early 17th century to the mid-20th century. Richard Frank (1698-1762) obtained plans for a new house from James Paine and other architects in the 1750's but they were unexecuted. Frank was Recorder of Pontefract and Doncaster, one of the first Fellows of the Society of Antiquaries, and contemplated writing a West Riding history. His impressive collection of manuscripts, his own writings, and the collection of manuscripts of Dr. Johnston of Pontefract, were in the library at Campsall. His nephew Bacon Frank (1739-1812) employed John Carr to remodel Campsall in 1762-64. It was a rather plain house, stuccoed, of two-and-a-half storeys, the bleak façades punctuated by many windows. Inside, the hall had a screen of two columns supporting a segmental arch. Over the staircase was an oval, glazed dome. William Lindley of Doncaster worked at Campsall c.1800, but possibly did no more than design a new entrance screen and lodges. In 1897 the owner was Frederick Bacon Frank, in 1922 his widow. After 1945 Campsall was converted into flats. It was demolished in 1983 after extensive vandalism and theft.

(1) Campsall Hall (Stan Longley)

(2) Campsall Hall (Doncaster Library)

CAMPSMOUNT,
Campsall

Campsmount, a new house on a hill west of Campsall, designed for Thomas Yarborough (1687-1772) by John Carr of York, was built in 1752-55. Yarborough had interests in landscape gardening as well as architecture. He commissioned designs from John Howgill in 1728, Henry Flitcroft in 1742 and James Paine in 1751 before he decided on Carr's design. He wrote that 'a plain regular building composed with all the beauty of order is beyond all carving and ornaments'. Campsmount was certainly plain externally, a five-bay, two-and-a-half storey house flanked by lower wings. Inside was more lavish decoration: a hall with a screen of columns, good marble chimneypieces and rich plasterwork in the principal rooms. Campsmount passed from Yarborough to his cousins, and in 1802 to their cousin George Cooke of Streetthorpe (later Edenthorpe, see p.63). It continued in the Cooke-Yarborough family until the 1930's, though it was recorded in 1922 as unoccuupied. The West Riding County Council bought it as a possible home for the mentally handicapped. It was used and abused by the army in the 1939-45 War. When the National Health Service started in 1948 the cost of repairing and converting Campsmount was too high. It was allowed to fall into ruin and was demolished in 1959. Askern Campsmount School occupies the site.

Campsmount (Doncaster Library)

Campsmount, dining room (Doncaster Library)

SANDALL GROVE,
Kirk Sandall

A 17th century house, Sandall Grove was the seat of the Rokeby family, and stood in an estate of 1000 acres. In 1776 Thomas Rokeby sold it to the Martins of Barnby Dun. Sandall Grove was reconstructed c.1800. Plain shallow bows on the garden front were a Regency feature. In the 1920's the firm of Pilkington Brothers, glass manufacturers, bought the estate. In 1966 Sandall was the residence of Dr. and Mrs. W.L. Patrick. It was afterwards demolished.

Sandall Grove (Doncaster Library)

HEXTHORPE HALL,
near Doncaster

Hexthorpe overlooked the River Don near Doncaster and was also near Sprotborough Hall. It was a small house which Doncaster Corporation ordered to be rebuilt in 1756 according to a plan by Rickard. Nineteenth century owners were the Ramsden family, of whom Captain Frank Ramsden served in the Napoleonic Wars and did not die until 1872; and his son Frank Ramsden (d.1903) was a barrister. Hexthorpe was sold in 1937 and was demolished for a housing estate. Dell Crescent stands on the site.

Hexthorpe Hall (Doncaster Library)

STAPLETON PARK,
Darrington

After a succession of owners in the early 18th century Stapleton was bought in 1762 by Edward Lascelles, later 1st Earl of Harewood.

Between 1762 and 1764 Stapleton was rebuilt to designs by John Carr of York. In 1789 Stapleton was sold to Charles, 16th Baron Stourton, and in 1800 to Robert, 9th Lord Petre. His son Edward Petre owned Stapleton 1816-34, and about 1820 he employed a little-known architect, William Cleave, to make alterations, including the Greek Doric entrance portico. Petre was a great horseracing man and his stables were very successful in 1820-30. Petre's horses won the St. Leger three years running, in 1827-29. Petre built new stables at Stapleton with a turret at the rear, where the Angelus bell was rung every evening. The stable interiors were adorned with paintings of horses, some by John Frederick Herring. Petre sold Stapleton to the Barton family. Henry J. Hope Barton was the owner in 1897. Stapleton was demolished c.1930.

(1) Stapleton Park (D. Sherborn)

(2) Stapleton Park, garden front (RCHME)

BARNBURGH HALL,
near Doncaster

An Elizabethan house with three gables, mullioned and transomed windows, much altered in the 18th century and later. John, son of Sir Thomas More, acquired Barnburgh through his marriage with the heiress of the Cresacre family. In 1897 it was the seat of John Hartop, and in 1922 of F.J.O. Montague. Frederick Dundas was the tenant. The 'tastefully laid-out grounds' were 'admirably kept'. Barnburgh was bought by the National Coal Board in 1947 and demolished in 1967 because of mining subsidence.

Barnburgh Hall (Doncaster Library)

ADWICK HALL,
Adwick-le-Street

Adwick was built in 1673 for Richard Washington. After 1700 it was bought by Anthony Eyre. A watercolour shows its 18th century appearance: traditional 17th century style, old-fashioned for 1673. In 1791 it was bought by George Wroughton, an Indian 'nabob', and remodelled by William Lindley of Doncaster. No illustrations of the remodelled house are known. By the 1820's it was a ladies' school, which closed in 1849. Adwick was ruinous by 1864, and demolished some time afterwards.

Adwick Park, by George Nicholson, 1824

SKELLOW GRANGE,
Burghwallis

Originally Newsome Grange, Skellow was a 17th century house remodelled in the 18th century, with a five-bay centre and two-bay wings. It was stuccoed. The house had many owners, from Darcy Rawson in 1707 to W.H. Humble, racehorse owner, in the 20th century. The contents were sold in 1964 and the estate was bought by a farmer. Much repair and alteration needed to be done, and Skellow Grange was demolished in 1964.

(1) Skellow Grange (RCHME)

(2) BELOW RIGHT: Skellow Grange, aerial view (Doncaster Library)

BILHAM HOUSE,
Hickleton

No illustrations are known of Bilham, seat of the Hewitt family, demolished in c.1860. In the early 18th century it was owned by Thomas Selwood (d.1758) who remodelled the house and landscaped the grounds. It passed to his relative Selwood Hewitt (d.1789) and to his sons Thomas and William, in whose time a beautiful prospect-tower, designed by John Rawsthorne, was built in the grounds. Bilham was bought by trustees under the famous will of Peter Thelusson of Brodsworth, and tenanted in the 1820's by the Marquess (later 1st Duke) of Cleveland.

CARR HOUSE,
Doncaster

Hugh Childers, Mayor of Doncaster, built Carr House in 1604. The modest five-bay front received new windows in the 18th century. In 1884 Carr House was sold to Doncaster Council by R.H. Cooper. It was used as a fever hospital. In the 1960's, when no longer required, it was destroyed by fire. The area is now Carr House Road.

(1) Carr House (Doncaster Library)

(2) BELOW RIGHT: Carr House in flames, 1960's (Doncaster Library)

MICKLEGATE HOUSE,
Pontefract

Like John Milne's house at Wakefield, Micklegate House was a superior town house, 18th century, 5 bays, three storeys, with single-storey 3 bay wings added later. It had good plasterwork, one room having a ceiling which could have been by Giuseppe Cortese.

CROOKHILL,
Conisborough

Crookhill was a mid-18th century house of the Woodyeare family. Its curious front with awkward squared pilasters resembled, on a smaller scale, Walton Hall near Wakefield. In the early 20th century it was the home of Joseph Humble, who owned Askern Colliery, sunk in 1911. Crookhill was sold to the West Riding County Council in 1926. In 1948 it became a santorium for sufferers from tuberculosis, part of Doncaster hospitals, and with the decline of TB it was closed in 1963.

While empty it was damaged by vandals and was destroyed by fire in 1967. The grounds are a golf course for Doncaster.

Crookhill (R. Hayhurst)

FINNINGLEY PARK,
Austerfield

A mid-eighteenth century house for the Harvey family. It was a square, three-storey block with a long service wing. In 1897 John Spofforth Lister was the owner, in 1922 Frederick Parker Rhodes. In the 1939-45 War Finningley was requisitioned by the RAF. Afterwards the site was used for quarrying, and by 1959 Pevsner described Finningley as 'overlooking a desert of sand and gravel digging'. It was demolished soon after. An airfield now covers the site.

Finningley Park (Doncaster Library)

RAVENFIELD,
near Doncaster

Ravenfield was destroyed by fire in 1963 after having been abandoned and derelict for several years. It was an eighteenth century building given its final form by John Carr of York in about 1760. The Wesby family had Ravenfield from the early seventeenth century until Wardell Wesby sold it to Mrs Elizabeth Parkin (1703-66) in 1749. The two wings on the north side, with their oversized gables punctuated with circular windows, probably dated from the Wesby period. The south side was more conventional, probably originally seven bays, but was extended on the west side by another three bays. Carr added the polygonal centre on the north side, which contained an octagonal drawing

(1) Ravenfield, entrance front (Mrs Springfield)

(2) Ravenfield, rear elevation (Mrs Springfield)

(3) Ravenfield, with John Carr's Ravenfield Church (Doncaster Library)

room. After Mrs Parkin's death the house passed through various hands until in about 1820 it came to James Birch (Bosville) of Thorpe Hall, Lincolnshire.

Ravenfield was last occupied in the 1920's.

(4) Ravenfield, entrance hall (Mrs Springfield

(5) Ravenfield, drawing room (Mrs Springfield)

SPROTBOROUGH HALL,
Doncaster

Sprotborough was dramatically sited on a high ridge on the south side of the River Don. The Copleys acquired the estate in the 16th century by marriage with an heiress of the previous family. Godfrey Copley, a Royalist, paid the large sum of £1,543 as a composition to keep Sprotborough after the Civil Wars. He was created a baronet in 1661. His son, Sir Godfrey Copley, was a scientist and an early member of the Royal Society. He built Sprotborough Hall in about 1696-1700, a square, restrained block of three storeys with a high parapet. John Etty of York, master-carpenter, had a hand in the building. The long wings were added soon after, since they are shown in paintings of the house c.1700 and in Samuel Buck's sketch of c.1720. On the entrance front the wings came forward to form a courtyard, and at the corners were two slender towers crowned with arched cupolas. Sir Godfrey Copley visited Versailles in 1685, and the lay-out of the house is said to have reflected, in a small way, Louis XIV's palace. Formal Dutch-style gardens ran down to the River Don. The internal decoration was by the painter Henry Cooke. About 1750 James Paine carried out some alterations for Godfrey Copley, but otherwise Sprotborough was little changed from 1700. On the death

(1) Sprotborough Hall, garden front (RCHME)

(2) Sprotborough Hall, entrance front and gatepiers (Doncaster Library)

of Sir Godfrey Copley in 1709 Sprotborough passed to his relation Lionel Copley, but after the death of Lionel Copley's second son in 1766 the estate passed to Joseph Moyle, a grandson of Sir Godfrey Copley. He assumed the name Copley and was created a baronet in 1778. His descendants held Sprotborough until the death of Sir Joseph Copley in 1882. Sir Charles Watson, a descendant in the female line of the Moyle Copleys, inherited, and changed his name to Copley. In 1897 it was the seat of Mrs. Bewicke-Copley. A succession of deaths in the Bewicke-Copley family in the early 20th century, with high death duties, led to the sale of the fine furnishings and valuable library in the early 1920's, and the house was demolished in 1926. The parkland was used for building houses.

(3) Sprotborough Hall, entrance front (Doncaster Library)

(4) Sprotborough Hall, hall and staircase (Country Life)

HATFIELD HOUSE,
near Doncaster

The residence of John Hatfield, captain of the Parliamentary army in the 1640's, Hatfield was refronted in the mid-18th century, in brick, in standard Palladian style. Hatfield had many resident families, including the Smiths, c.1890-1929, who moved to Sprotborough, and Lord Moncrieff, who moved in after the Edenthorpe fire. He later went to live on his estate in Scotland. The Army and Air Force had it in 1939-45 and afterwards, despite the local council's idea to turn it into flats, the estate was sold in 1952, and Hatfield was demolished in 1955. New houses stand on the site.

Hatfield House (Doncaster Library)

HOOTON LEVITT HALL,
Maltby

A square Georgian house of three bays. On the entrance front, semicircular walls projected forward, ending in urns. The balustraded parapet was probably a 19th century addition. In the late 19th century a 'half-timbered' range was added at the back of the house. In the 19th century the lawyer William Hoyle (1801-86) inherited the estate. He was solicitor to the Earl of Effingham and steward of the Manor of Rotherham. Hooton Levitt was demolished in 1964. Modern housing now covers the site.

Hooton Levitt Hall (Rotherham Library)

GREAT HOUGHTON HALL,
near Darfield

The seat of the Rodes family was a substantial 16th century house, H-shaped, the main entrance on the south side (to the right in the Gott drawing) and a central entrance on the west side approached up an impressive flight of steps. The windows all had mullions and transoms. It remained in the Rodes family until the death of Mrs. Mary Rodes in 1789. It was bought by Richard Slater Milnes who found its picturesque interiors very primitive and inconvenient, and spent £1000 on alterations. Immediately he let it to tenants and moved to Fryston Hall. By 1828 it had become a public house, but its exterior was little altered until it was gutted by fire in 1960 and demolished.

(1) Great Houghton Hall (Wakefield Art Gallery, Gott Collection)

(2) Great Houghton Hall, east front (RCHME)

WHEATLEY HALL,
Doncaster

The seat of the Cooke family for 250 years, Wheatley was demolished in 1934. It was built for Sir Henry Cooke, 2nd Baronet, about 1680, an ambitious early classical house of nine bays, three and a half storeys, and slightly more windows to wall than was usual. Kelly's *Directory* spoke of 'a profusion of windows'. In the entrance hall was a magnificent carved staircase, in oak, elm and pine, with a swirling foliage motif instead of balusters - perhaps carved by Grinling Gibbons or a pupil. When Wheatley was demolished the staircase was bought by Sir Paul Latham and installed in Hurstmonceux Castle in Sussex. Downstairs was a large drawing room, upstairs a French drawing room and a tapestry room. The last Cooke baronet to live at Wheatley was Sir William Wemyss Cooke until c.1910. He moved to Berkshire.

(1) Wheatley Hall (S. Longley)

(2) Wheatley Hall, lower drawing room (P.P. Davies-Cooke)

Wheatley was in military use in the 1914-18 War, and afterwards, with its 103 acres of park landscaped by White, it was leased by Wheatley Park Golf Club. The upper floors were turned into flats. The Hall was sold to Doncaster Council in 1933 for £60,000, and was demolished in 1934. The site is now in industrial use, by Du Ponts and J.I. Case Ltd.

(3) Wheatley Hall, staircase (P.P. Davies-Cooke)

HOOTON ROBERTS HALL, near Rotherham

Hooton Roberts Hall, a late 16th or early 17th century house of two storeys, with four full-height bowed bays on the main front. It was a seat of Thomas Wentworth, Earl of Strafford (1593-1641), minister of Charles I. His widow lived at Hooton Roberts for some years after his death. The Hall was illustrated in an early 18th century engraving, but was subsequently demolished.

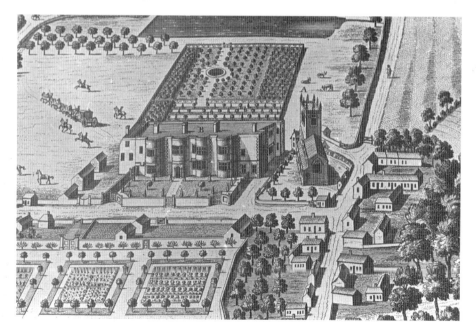

Hooton Roberts (detail of a print after 1728 attributed to John Settrington)

ALDWARKE HALL,
near Rotherham

The 17th century seat of the Foljambe family is illustrated in a drawing in the Gott collection. It was a long, many-gabled range with late-Gothic windows including an oriel, and a central, projecting porch. Aldwarke was rebuilt c.1720 for Francis Foljambe. It was a handsome, H-shaped house of three storeys, of stone, plain classical, with a later balustraded parapet and corner urns. James Wyatt remodelled the interiors for Francis Foljambe in 1773-75, and numerous plans survive, that for the dining room matching a photograph of a corner of the room. Aldwarke was demolished in 1899.

(1) Aldwarke Hall, old house (Wakefield Art Gallery, Gott Collection)

(2) Aldwarke Hall, garden front (G. Foljambe)

(3) Aldwarke Hall, dining room (G. Foljambe)

THORPE SALVIN
MANOR HOUSE

Thorpe Salvin, long ruined, so that only the gatehouse and main façade survive, was designed by Robert Smythson for Henry Sandford in the 1570's. It was a three storey house, symmetrical, with a central rectangular porch bay, two massive chimney stacks, and round corner towers. There were round towers on the other side also. Thorpe Salvin was sold to Sir Edward Osborne in 1636. He was a Royalist, and the house was stormed in the Civil war by Parliamentarians and partly demolished.

Thorpe Salvin (R. Hayhurst)

DODWORTH HALL,
near Barnsley

A little-known house, the centre, with its portico and small pediment possibly c.1800, the taller and not quite symmetrical wings a little later. Kelly in 1897 recorded it as 'delightfully seated on an eminence to the west of the village, commanding fine prospects', but 'vacant'; and it was still 'unoccupied' in the 1922 edition of Kelly.

Dodworth Hall (J. Davidson)

ICKLES HALL,
Rotherham

A manor-house of c.1600 on the site of an older house, with many gables and tall chimneys. It was built for Thomas Reresby, and afterwards his mother, Lady Reresby, a devout catholic, lived there. Services were held in a large room, used as a chapel. From about 1900 Ickles was a farmhouse, owned by Hannah Wood and occupied by the Picken family. It was demolished in 1939. United Steels bought the site and it was built over.

(1) Ickles Hall (Rotherham Library, Archives and Local Studies)

(2) Ickles Hall (Rotherham Library, Archives and Local Studies)

EASTWOOD HOUSE,
Rotherham

Designed by John Carr in 1786-87 for Joseph Walker. Eastwood was a good classical house with the common Carr feature of a canted bay. Walker's son Samuel was a close friend of William Wilberforce. There were several 19th century owners, the last being George Neill. Eastwood was sold in 1920, and the grounds were taken for housing development. The house was demolished in 1928. A new house was built on the site, which later became a residential home.

Eastwood House (Rotherham Library, Archives and Local Studies)

GAWBER HALL,
near Barnsley

Gawber Hall, an ancient manor house with a centre and two wings, one half-timbered, the other of stone, has been demolished. In 1897 it was the home of John Brown, farmer.

Gawber Hall (J. Davidson)

83

WOMBWELL HALL,
near Barnsley

Wombwell Hall, a large manor-house part medieval, part 17th century, with some 18th century alterations, was the seat of the Wombwell family from the late 13th to the 18th century. The last in the senior male line was William Wombwell (1700-33), whose two daughters were co-heiresses. The manor and estate were offered for sale in large or small blocks. A cousin, Sir George Wombwell, an Indian 'nabob', bought most of the estate but did not live at the hall. It was let to tenants, and fell into decay. In 1881 when Joseph Wilkinson wrote, it was divided and very dilapidated, and was demolished some time later.

Wombwell Hall

NETHERWOOD HALL,
Wombwell

Netherwood, one of several small seats at Wombwell, was in ruins when the photograph was taken in 1964. It was a distinguished early 18th century house of seven bays, with a three-bay pediment and a segmental-headed doorcase. In 1897 Arthur Garland was the occupier, in 1922 John Halmshaw.

Netherwood Hall (RCHME)

KIVETON HALL

Kiveton, the south Yorkshire seat of the Dukes of Leeds, was demolished in 1812. The Dukes had also Hornby Castle near Bedale (see *Lost Houses of York and the North Riding*). Kiveton was built in 1694-1704 for Thomas Osborne, 1st Duke of Leeds (1620-1712). William Talman was consulted and made designs, but the Hall was executed by an unknown architect. Amongst the craftsmen employed was Jean Tijou the ironsmith. Louis Hauduroy did much decorative painting at Kiveton, and Sir James Thornhill painted the hall.

THE FRONT of *Kiveton House* the SEAT of *his Grace* THOMAS OSBORNE *DUKE*
MARQUIS *of* Carmarthen EARL *of* Danby VISCOUNT Latimer & Dumblan BARON Osborne *of* Kiveton & Baronet

Kiveton Hall (Vitruvius Britannicus, iv, 1739)

THE FARM,
Sheffield

The Dukes of Norfolk owned much of Sheffield, but until the succession of the 14th Duke in 1856 they rarely visited the town. The 14th Duke commissioned local architects Weightman, Hadfield and Goldie to adapt a farmhouse for his occasional use. Extensively transformed in a Tudor style, with a tall tower and a gateway with a private chapel over it, The Farm quickly suffered from a railway tunnel under the garden in 1869, and in 1899 it was sold to the Midland Railway. It was demolished in 1967

The Farm, Sheffield

BIBLIOGRAPHY

A series of picturesque views of castles and country houses in Yorkshire, Bradford, 1885

S.O. Addy, *Sheffield and neighbourhood at the opening of the 20th century. Contemporary biographies,* (W.T. Pike, ed.), 1901

Louis Ambler, *The Old Halls and Manor Houses of Yorkshire,* 1913

John Ayers, *Architecture in Bradford,* 1972

W.S. Banks, *Walks in Yorkshire: Wakefield and its neighbourhood,* 1871

Clyde Binfield *et al.,* (ed.), *The history of the City of Sheffield 1843-1993,* 1993

Buck's Yorkshire sketchbook, Wakefield Historical Publications, 1980

[John Carr]. *The works in architecture of John Carr,* York Georgian Society, 1973

H.M. Colvin, *A biographical dictionary of British architects 1660-1840,* 3rd ed., 1995

Timothy Connor, 'The building of Campsmount', *Yorkshire Archaeological Journal,* 47, 1975

Country Life magazine:
  Methley Hall, 18 May 1907
  Byram Hall, 9 June 1917
  'Sprotborough Hall, Doncaster. The seat of Brig.-Gen. Sir A.
  Bewicke-Copley', 11 February 1922
  Christopher Hussey, `Studley Royal, Yorkshire. The seat of Mr. Clare Vyner', 25 July - 1 August 1931

W. Cudworth, *Round about Bradford; a series of sketches,* 1876

W. Cudworth, *The history of Manningham, Heaton and Allerton,* 1896

J.S. Fletcher, *Memorials of a Yorkshire parish. An historical sketch of the parish of Darrington,* 1917

John Gilleghan, *Highways and Byways from Leeds,* 1994

John Gilleghan, *Scenes from East Leeds,* 1992

Mark Girouard, *Robert Smythson and the Elizabethan country house,* 1983

Lady Green, *The old hall at Heath, 1568-1888,* 1889

Halifax Antiquarian Society *Transactions*

Joseph Hunter, *South Yorkshire,* 1828

John James, *The history and topography of Bradford,* 1841

Kelly's Directory of the West Riding of Yorkshire, various editions 1897-1922

Peter Leach, *James Paine,* 1988

Derek Linstrum, *West Yorkshire. Architects and architecture,* 1978.

John Nussey, 'Blake Hall, in Mirfield, and its occupants during the 18th and 19th centuries', *Yorkshire Archaeological Journal,* 55, 1983

N. Pevsner, *The buildings of England: Yorkshire West Riding* 2nd ed., 1967

David Pickersgill, *A History of Byram Hall and Park,* 1996

SAVE Britain's Heritage, *Vanishing Houses of England,* 1982

W.H. Scott, *The West Riding of Yorkshire at the opening of the 20th century. Contemporary biographies,* (W.T. Pike, ed.), 1902

William Scruton, *Pen and pencil pictures of old Bradford,* 1899

George Sheeran, *Brass Castles. West Yorkshire new rich and their houses 1800-1914,* 1993

George Sheeran, *Good houses built of stone. The houses and people of Leeds / Bradford 1600-1800,* 1986

Gordon Smith, articles on Doncaster and district houses in *Doncaster Gazette and Journal,* c.1965-67

Gordon Smith, *Catalogue of a pictorial exhibition of the country houses of Doncaster and district,* 1992

William Smith, *Morley ancient and modern, 1886*

Harry Speight, *Craven and the north-west Yorkshire highlands,* 1892

Harry Speight, *Chronicles and stories of old Bingley,* 1899

Harry Speight, *Upper Nidderdale, with the Forest of Knaresborough,* 1906

Harry Speight, *Lower Wharfedale,* 1902

Roy Strong, Marcus Binney, John Harris, *The Destruction of the Country House,* 1974

Angus Taylor, 'William Lindley of Doncaster' *Georgian Group Journal,* 1994

Vernon Thornes, *Historic houses in Rotherham district,* 1989

T.D. Whitaker, *History and antiquities of the Deanery of Craven,* 1812

T.D. Whitaker, *Leodis and Elmet,* 1816

ACKNOWLEDGEMENTS

Inevitably in such a large county, help came from so many quarters that it is not possible to mention them all by name. We would, however, like to thank in particular Jim Davidson, Bob Hayhurst, Angus Taylor, Gordon Smith, Philip Meadows, Brian Elliott, Derek Linstrum, Maxwell Craven, John Gilleghan, David Pickering and Peter Reid.

Numerous institutions and dozens of unsung heroes in the form of local studies librarians have been of immeasurable help in searching for and providing material. We are especially grateful to the Royal Commission on the Historical Monuments of England for supplying so many of the illustrations, Doncaster Library and Information Services, including the Gordon Smith Collection; the City of Bradford Metropolitan Council, Arts, Museums and Libraries Division, Rotherham Borough Council, Archives and Local Studies Section; pictures of The Knoll, Baildon and Shelf Hall are reproduced by kind permission of the Telegraph & Argus, Bradford and to Jill Waterson for her help and encouragement throughout this series of books.

Finally, we were greatly honoured when John Harris kindly agreed to write the foreword. Had it not been for his critically influential 1974 exhibition *The Destruction of the Country House* this book would have never seen the light of day.

Edward Waterson
Carter Jonas
York

Peter Meadows
Cambridge University Library
Cambridge

1998

INDEX